A WRITER'S JOURNAL AND WORKBOOK

KAREN PEPIN

JKCB Press LLC
PO Box 710, Lorton, VA 22199

First edition, 2022.
ISBN-13:   978-1-7328142-8-8 (Hardcover)
ISBN-13:   978-1-953061-10-2 (Paperback)

Printed in the United States of America.

JKCB Press LLC
PO Box 710
Lorton, VA 22199

www.KarenPepin.com

To my husband, Jason

ABOUT THIS JOURNAL

Many writers use computer programs to keep all their story information in one place. However, I have always written my story prep work by hand. It allows me to really play around with an idea and grow it. World Building, characters, plot – all these I find easier to do if I simply write in a journal. Plus, I can more easily carry a journal around than my computer for jotting down thoughts when they strike.

Unfortunately, this causes me to have tons of journals with a mishmash of multiple stories in them, making it hard to remain organized and avoid misplacing things. Recently, I ran across a YouTube video regarding creating low content books, particularly journals. I thought, I don't really want to get into the low content market creating journals, but what if I simply make a journal for me to use to help organize my novel writing from the starting ideas through the first draft. So I did.

This journal is NOT a guide of how to plot a novel. It's more like a workbook with tips that have helped me over the years of writing. I'm not a plotter by nature. I'm more of a "plantser," someone who does some plotting but writes a great deal by the seat of my pants. This workbook gives me the space to do that.

So how does this journal work and what's in it? I have organized it by sections.

Ideas:
The first question I ask myself when coming up with a story is "What If." But, I have found that coming up with really good ideas can take many tries. So, this section has space for that. My idea, pun intended, is to spend some time coming up with multiple ideas. Then I choose the strongest idea, one that appeals to me the most, to continue developing into a novel.

Setting and World Building:
This is just a section to come up with as much or as little as you need for your story. If writing Science Fiction, you need to consider modes of travel and their effects on the characters. In Fantasy, magic use requires rules to make sense for the reader. This section is where you can flesh all those things out.

Characters:
Making the characters, both heroes and villains, relatable requires delving deep into who they are and what they want.

Plot:
There are many ways to plot out a story- Three act story, Hero's Journey, Snowflake method. This workbook isn't meant to teach those. There are three parts to my Plot section. The Short Synopsis gives space for a 2-3 sentence idea for a chapter. The Expanded Chapter Breakdown delves more into the intro hook, the basic tension/action for that chapter and the ending hook. The last part is the First Draft. I like to have the full basic plot planned out so I know where I'm going before drafting. Some people simply write and cobble the story together in the end. I began writing by doing that myself. But, I have discovered that, for me, knowing the major plot points and direction I'm going helps me keep momentum while writing.

Research:
As the name implies, it is just an area for you to write down the items you have researched for this story. This section also has blank pages for maps if you want to design one. I am not much of an artist, but being able to map out a city or a world or a space station, etc… helps me visualized the places I'm writing about.

Some people prefer focusing on Characters first; others on Setting. I organized this journal for what works for me. But, start with what works best for you. Play around with your story and ideas. I hope this workbook helps you grow your novel. Happy writing!

Section One: Ideas

TIP #1

Potential story ideas are everywhere. Just keep your eyes and ears open. Keep asking, "What if." Who knows where it will take you.

What If:

_____

_____

_____

_____

_____

_____

_____

What If:

_____

_____

_____

_____

_____

_____

_____

What If:

_____

_____

_____

_____

_____

_____

What If:

_____

_____

_____

_____

_____

_____

What If:

_____

_____

_____

_____

_____

_____

What If:

_____

_____

_____

_____

_____

_____

What If:

_____

_____

_____

_____

_____

_____

What If:

_____

_____

_____

_____

_____

_____

What If:

_____

_____

_____

_____

_____

_____

_____

What If:

_____

_____

_____

_____

_____

_____

_____

What If:

_____

_____

_____

_____

_____

_____

What If:

_____

_____

_____

_____

_____

_____

IDEAS

What If:

_____

_____

_____

_____

_____

_____

_____

What If:

_____

_____

_____

_____

_____

_____

_____

IDEAS

What If:

_____

_____

_____

_____

_____

_____

_____

What If:

_____

_____

_____

_____

_____

_____

_____

What If:

_____

_____

_____

_____

_____

_____

What If:

_____

_____

_____

_____

_____

_____

What If:

_____

_____

_____

_____

_____

_____

What If:

_____

_____

_____

_____

_____

_____

What If:

_____

_____

_____

_____

_____

_____

What If:

_____

_____

_____

_____

_____

_____

What If:

_____

_____

_____

_____

_____

_____

What If:

_____

_____

_____

_____

_____

_____

What If:

_____

_____

_____

_____

_____

_____

What If:

_____

_____

_____

_____

_____

_____

What If:

_____

_____

_____

_____

_____

_____

What If:

_____

_____

_____

_____

_____

_____

What If:

_____

_____

_____

_____

_____

_____

_____

What If:

_____

_____

_____

_____

_____

_____

_____

What If:

_____

_____

_____

_____

_____

_____

What If:

_____

_____

_____

_____

_____

_____

IDEAS

What If:

_____

_____

_____

_____

_____

_____

What If:

_____

_____

_____

_____

_____

_____

What If:

_____

_____

_____

_____

_____

_____

What If:

_____

_____

_____

_____

_____

_____

IDEAS

What If:

_____

_____

_____

_____

_____

_____

What If:

_____

_____

_____

_____

_____

_____

What If:

_____

_____

_____

_____

_____

_____

What If:

_____

_____

_____

_____

_____

_____

What If:

_____

_____

_____

_____

_____

_____

What If:

_____

_____

_____

_____

_____

_____

What If:

_____

_____

_____

_____

_____

What If:

_____

_____

_____

_____

_____

_____

What If:

_____

_____

_____

_____

_____

_____

What If:

_____

_____

_____

_____

_____

_____

What If:

_____

_____

_____

_____

_____

_____

What If:

_____

_____

_____

_____

_____

_____

What If:

_____

_____

_____

_____

_____

_____

_____

What If:

_____

_____

_____

_____

_____

_____

_____

IDEAS

What If:

_____

_____

_____

_____

_____

_____

What If:

_____

_____

_____

_____

_____

_____

What If:

_____

_____

_____

_____

_____

_____

What If:

_____

_____

_____

_____

_____

_____

What If:

_____

_____

_____

_____

_____

_____

What If:

_____

_____

_____

_____

_____

_____

What If:

_____

_____

_____

_____

_____

_____

_____

What If:

_____

_____

_____

_____

_____

_____

_____

IDEAS

What If:

_____

_____

_____

_____

_____

_____

What If:

_____

_____

_____

_____

_____

_____

What If:

_____

_____

_____

_____

_____

_____

What If:

_____

_____

_____

_____

_____

_____

Section Two: World Building / Setting

TIP #2

Always consider the society your characters live in from the small details, such as food and daily survival, to the larger ones, such as Politics, Laws, and Religion. Think about how these things will affect character interactions.

In Science Fiction, consider the science of things like means of travel. Does your character travel on a generational ship or one that travels faster than light (FTL)? How does either mode affect how the characters' lives?

In Fantasy, consider the various traits of the races. If you include magic, remember that magic will also be governed by rules.

The more detailed you create your world, the more immersive it'll be for the reader. The sky is the limit. Be creative. Just remember it also has to be grounded in rules to make sense to the reader.

Setting / World Building

_____

_____

_____

_____

_____

_____

_____

_____

_____

_____

_____

_____

_____

_____

Setting / World Building

_____

_____

_____

_____

_____

_____

_____

_____

_____

_____

_____

_____

_____

Setting / World Building

_____

_____

_____

_____

_____

_____

_____

_____

_____

_____

_____

_____

_____

_____

Setting / World Building

_____

_____

_____

_____

_____

_____

_____

_____

_____

_____

_____

_____

_____

Setting / World Building

_____

_____

_____

_____

_____

_____

_____

_____

_____

_____

_____

_____

_____

_____

Setting / World Building

_____

_____

_____

_____

_____

_____

_____

_____

_____

_____

_____

_____

_____

Setting / World Building

_____

_____

_____

_____

_____

_____

_____

_____

_____

_____

_____

_____

_____

_____

_____

Setting / World Building

_____

_____

_____

_____

_____

_____

_____

_____

_____

_____

_____

_____

_____

Setting / World Building

Setting / World Building

Setting / World Building

_____

_____

_____

_____

_____

_____

_____

_____

_____

_____

_____

_____

_____

_____

Setting / World Building

Setting / World Building

_____

_____

_____

_____

_____

_____

_____

_____

_____

_____

_____

_____

_____

Setting / World Building

_____

_____

_____

_____

_____

_____

_____

_____

_____

_____

_____

_____

_____

Setting / World Building

Setting / World Building

_____

_____

_____

_____

_____

_____

_____

_____

_____

_____

_____

_____

_____

_____

Setting / World Building

Setting / World Building

_____

_____

_____

_____

_____

_____

_____

_____

_____

_____

_____

_____

_____

Setting / World Building

Setting / World Building

Setting / World Building

_____

_____

_____

_____

_____

_____

_____

_____

_____

_____

_____

_____

_____

Setting / World Building

_____

_____

_____

_____

_____

_____

_____

_____

_____

_____

_____

_____

_____

Setting / World Building

_____

_____

_____

_____

_____

_____

_____

_____

_____

_____

_____

_____

_____

_____

Setting / World Building

_____

_____

_____

_____

_____

_____

_____

_____

_____

_____

_____

_____

_____

Setting / World Building

Setting / World Building

_____

_____

_____

_____

_____

_____

_____

_____

_____

_____

_____

_____

_____

Setting / World Building

_____

_____

_____

_____

_____

_____

_____

_____

_____

_____

_____

_____

_____

_____

Setting / World Building

_____

_____

_____

_____

_____

_____

_____

_____

_____

_____

_____

_____

_____

_____

Setting / World Building

_____

_____

_____

_____

_____

_____

_____

_____

_____

_____

_____

_____

_____

_____

Setting / World Building

_____

_____

_____

_____

_____

_____

_____

_____

_____

_____

_____

_____

_____

Setting / World Building

Section Three: Characters

TIP #3

Give your characters flaws and fears. They can face their fears to grow. They can turn their flaws into strengths if they are brave enough. Everyone has some thing about themselves that they don't like. Characters should too.

CHARACTERS

Character Name:

_____

Description:

_____

_____

_____

_____

_____

Back Story:

_____

_____

_____

_____

_____

_____

CHARACTERS

Flaws / Strengths:

_____

_____

_____

_____

_____

Wants:

_____

_____

_____

_____

_____

_____

_____

Needs:

_____

_____

_____

_____

_____

_____

Fears:

_____

_____

_____

_____

_____

_____

_____

CHARACTERS

Character Name:

_____

Description:

_____

_____

_____

_____

_____

_____

Back Story:

_____

_____

_____

_____

_____

_____

CHARACTERS

Flaws / Strengths:

_____

_____

_____

_____

_____

_____

Wants:

_____

_____

_____

_____

_____

_____

_____

_____

Needs:

_____

_____

_____

_____

_____

_____

Fears:

_____

_____

_____

_____

_____

_____

_____

CHARACTERS

Character Name:

_____

Description:

_____

_____

_____

_____

_____

_____

Back Story:

_____

_____

_____

_____

_____

_____

CHARACTERS

Flaws / Strengths:

_____

_____

_____

_____

_____

_____

Wants:

_____

_____

_____

_____

_____

_____

_____

Needs:

_____

_____

_____

_____

_____

Fears:

_____

_____

_____

_____

_____

_____

CHARACTERS

Character Name:

_____

Description:

_____

_____

_____

_____

_____

_____

Back Story:

_____

_____

_____

_____

_____

_____

CHARACTERS

Flaws / Strengths:

_____

_____

_____

_____

_____

_____

Wants:

_____

_____

_____

_____

_____

_____

_____

_____

CHARACTERS

Needs:

_____

_____

_____

_____

_____

_____

Fears:

_____

_____

_____

_____

_____

_____

_____

Character Name:

_____

Description:

_____

_____

_____

_____

_____

_____

Back Story:

_____

_____

_____

_____

_____

CHARACTERS

Flaws / Strengths:

_____

_____

_____

_____

_____

_____

Wants:

_____

_____

_____

_____

_____

_____

_____

Needs:

_____

_____

_____

_____

_____

_____

Fears:

_____

_____

_____

_____

_____

_____

_____

CHARACTERS

Character Name:

_____

Description:

_____

_____

_____

_____

_____

_____

Back Story:

_____

_____

_____

_____

_____

_____

CHARACTERS

Flaws / Strengths:

_____

_____

_____

_____

_____

Wants:

_____

_____

_____

_____

_____

_____

_____

_____

Needs:

_____

_____

_____

_____

_____

_____

Fears:

_____

_____

_____

_____

_____

_____

_____

CHARACTERS

Character Name:

_____

Description:

_____

_____

_____

_____

_____

_____

Back Story:

_____

_____

_____

_____

_____

CHARACTERS

Flaws / Strengths:

_____

_____

_____

_____

_____

_____

Wants:

_____

_____

_____

_____

_____

_____

_____

_____

Needs:

_____

_____

_____

_____

_____

_____

_____

Fears:

_____

_____

_____

_____

_____

_____

_____

CHARACTERS

Character Name:

_____

Description:

_____

_____

_____

_____

_____

_____

Back Story:

_____

_____

_____

_____

_____

_____

CHARACTERS

Flaws / Strengths:

_____

_____

_____

_____

_____

_____

Wants:

_____

_____

_____

_____

_____

_____

_____

_____

Needs:

_____

_____

_____

_____

_____

_____

Fears:

_____

_____

_____

_____

_____

_____

_____

Character Name:

_____

Description:

_____

_____

_____

_____

_____

_____

Back Story:

_____

_____

_____

_____

_____

_____

CHARACTERS

Flaws / Strengths:

_____

_____

_____

_____

_____

_____

Wants:

_____

_____

_____

_____

_____

_____

_____

_____

Needs:

_____

_____

_____

_____

_____

_____

Fears:

_____

_____

_____

_____

_____

_____

_____

CHARACTERS

Character Name:

_____

Description:

_____

_____

_____

_____

_____

_____

Back Story:

_____

_____

_____

_____

_____

_____

CHARACTERS

Flaws / Strengths:

_____

_____

_____

_____

_____

_____

Wants:

_____

_____

_____

_____

_____

_____

_____

CHARACTERS

Needs:

_____

_____

_____

_____

_____

_____

Fears:

_____

_____

_____

_____

_____

_____

_____

Section Four: Plot

TIP #4

Raise the stakes. While plotting and writing, always consider how to keep the tension or action high.

TIP #5

Make things hard for your characters. A story where everything comes easily to the main character is boring. A character needs to face adversity to grow.

Plot

Chapter One

_____

_____

_____

_____

_____

_____

_____

Chapter Two

_____

_____

_____

_____

_____

_____

_____

Plot

Chapter Three

_____

_____

_____

_____

_____

_____

Chapter Four

_____

_____

_____

_____

_____

_____

Chapter Five

_____

_____

_____

_____

_____

_____

_____

Chapter Six

_____

_____

_____

_____

_____

_____

_____

Plot

Chapter Seven

_____

_____

_____

_____

_____

Chapter Eight

_____

_____

_____

_____

_____

Chapter Nine

Chapter Ten

Plot

Short Synopsis

Chapter Eleven

Chapter Twelve

Plot

Chapter Thirteen

_____

_____

_____

_____

_____

_____

Chapter Fourteen

_____

_____

_____

_____

_____

_____

Plot

Chapter Fifteen

_____

_____

_____

_____

_____

_____

Chapter Sixteen

_____

_____

_____

_____

_____

_____

Chapter Seventeen

_____

_____

_____

_____

_____

Chapter Eighteen

_____

_____

_____

_____

_____

Plot

Chapter Nineteen

_____

_____

_____

_____

_____

Chapter Twenty

_____

_____

_____

_____

_____

Chapter Twenty-One

_____

_____

_____

_____

_____

_____

_____

Chapter Twenty-Two

_____

_____

_____

_____

_____

_____

Plot

Chapter Twenty-Three

_____

_____

_____

_____

_____

Chapter Twenty-Four

_____

_____

_____

_____

_____

Plot

Chapter Twenty-Five

Chapter Twenty-Six

Plot

Chapter Twenty-Seven

_____

_____

_____

_____

_____

Chapter Twenty-Eight

_____

_____

_____

_____

_____

Plot

Chapter Twenty-Nine

Chapter Thirty

Expanded Chapter Breakdown

Opening Hook:

_____

_____

_____

_____

Action or Tension of this Chapter

_____

_____

_____

_____

Closing Hook:

_____

_____

_____

_____

Plot

Opening Hook:

_____

_____

_____

_____

Action or Tension of this Chapter

_____

_____

_____

_____

_____

Closing Hook:

_____

_____

_____

_____

_____

Plot

Opening Hook:

_____

_____

_____

_____

Action or Tension of this Chapter

_____

_____

_____

_____

_____

Closing Hook:

_____

_____

_____

_____

_____

Plot

Opening Hook:

_____

_____

_____

_____

Action or Tension of this Chapter

_____

_____

_____

_____

_____

Closing Hook:

_____

_____

_____

_____

_____

Plot

Opening Hook:

_____

_____

_____

_____

Action or Tension of this Chapter

_____

_____

_____

_____

_____

Closing Hook:

_____

_____

_____

_____

_____

Plot

Opening Hook:

_____

_____

_____

_____

Action or Tension of this Chapter

_____

_____

_____

_____

_____

Closing Hook:

_____

_____

_____

_____

_____

Plot

Opening Hook:

_____

_____

_____

_____

Action or Tension of this Chapter

_____

_____

_____

_____

Closing Hook:

_____

_____

_____

_____

Plot

Opening Hook:

_____

_____

_____

_____

Action or Tension of this Chapter

_____

_____

_____

_____

_____

Closing Hook:

_____

_____

_____

_____

Plot

Opening Hook:

_____

_____

_____

_____

Action or Tension of this Chapter

_____

_____

_____

_____

_____

Closing Hook:

_____

_____

_____

_____

_____

Plot

Opening Hook:

_____

_____

_____

_____

Action or Tension of this Chapter

_____

_____

_____

_____

_____

Closing Hook:

_____

_____

_____

_____

_____

Opening Hook:

_____

_____

_____

_____

Action or Tension of this Chapter

_____

_____

_____

_____

Closing Hook:

_____

_____

_____

_____

Plot

Opening Hook:

_____

_____

_____

_____

Action or Tension of this Chapter

_____

_____

_____

_____

_____

Closing Hook:

_____

_____

_____

_____

_____

Plot

Opening Hook:

_____

_____

_____

_____

Action or Tension of this Chapter

_____

_____

_____

_____

Closing Hook:

_____

_____

_____

_____

Plot

Opening Hook:

_____

_____

_____

_____

Action or Tension of this Chapter

_____

_____

_____

_____

_____

Closing Hook:

_____

_____

_____

_____

Chapter Fifteen

Opening Hook:

_____

_____

_____

_____

Action or Tension of this Chapter

_____

_____

_____

_____

_____

Closing Hook:

_____

_____

_____

_____

_____

Plot

Opening Hook:

_____

_____

_____

_____

Action or Tension of this Chapter

_____

_____

_____

_____

_____

Closing Hook:

_____

_____

_____

_____

Opening Hook:

_____

_____

_____

_____

Action or Tension of this Chapter

_____

_____

_____

_____

_____

Closing Hook:

_____

_____

_____

_____

Plot

Opening Hook:

_____

_____

_____

_____

Action or Tension of this Chapter

_____

_____

_____

_____

Closing Hook:

_____

_____

_____

_____

Chapter Nineteen

Plot

Opening Hook:

_____

_____

_____

_____

Action or Tension of this Chapter

_____

_____

_____

_____

Closing Hook:

_____

_____

_____

_____

Plot

Opening Hook:

_____

_____

_____

_____

Action or Tension of this Chapter

_____

_____

_____

_____

Closing Hook:

_____

_____

_____

_____

Opening Hook:

_____

_____

_____

_____

Action or Tension of this Chapter

_____

_____

_____

_____

_____

Closing Hook:

_____

_____

_____

_____

_____

Plot

Opening Hook:

_____

_____

_____

_____

Action or Tension of this Chapter

_____

_____

_____

_____

_____

Closing Hook:

_____

_____

_____

_____

Plot

Opening Hook:

_____

_____

_____

_____

Action or Tension of this Chapter

_____

_____

_____

_____

Closing Hook:

_____

_____

_____

_____

Plot

Opening Hook:

_____

_____

_____

_____

Action or Tension of this Chapter

_____

_____

_____

_____

_____

Closing Hook:

_____

_____

_____

_____

Opening Hook:

_____

_____

_____

_____

Action or Tension of this Chapter

_____

_____

_____

_____

Closing Hook:

_____

_____

_____

_____

Plot

Opening Hook:

_____

_____

_____

_____

Action or Tension of this Chapter

_____

_____

_____

_____

_____

Closing Hook:

_____

_____

_____

_____

Chapter Twenty-Seven

Plot

Opening Hook:

_____

_____

_____

_____

Action or Tension of this Chapter

_____

_____

_____

_____

_____

Closing Hook:

_____

_____

_____

_____

_____

Plot

Opening Hook:

_____

_____

_____

_____

Action or Tension of this Chapter

_____

_____

_____

_____

_____

Closing Hook:

_____

_____

_____

_____

Opening Hook:

_____

_____

_____

_____

Action or Tension of this Chapter

_____

_____

_____

_____

_____

Closing Hook:

_____

_____

_____

_____

_____

Plot

Opening Hook:

_____

_____

_____

_____

Action or Tension of this Chapter

_____

_____

_____

_____

_____

Closing Hook:

_____

_____

_____

_____

YOUR TIPS

What things do you want to remind
yourself while writing?

First
Draft

1st Draft

1st Draft

1st Draft

1st Draft

1st Draft

1st Draft

1st Draft

1st Draft

1st Draft

1st Draft

1st Draft

1st Draft

1st Draft

1st Draft

1st Draft

1st Draft

1st Draft

1st Draft

1st Draft

1st Draft

1st Draft

1st Draft

1st Draft

1st Draft

1st Draft

1st Draft

1st Draft

1st Draft

1st Draft

1st Draft

1st Draft

1st Draft

1st Draft

1st Draft

1st Draft

1st Draft

1st Draft

1ˢᵗ Draft

1st Draft

1st Draft

1st Draft

1st Draft

1ˢᵗ Draft

1st Draft

1st Draft

1st Draft

1st Draft

1st Draft

1st Draft

1st Draft

1st Draft

1st Draft

1st Draft

1st Draft

1st Draft

1st Draft

1st Draft

1st Draft

1st Draft

1st Draft

1st Draft

1st Draft

1st Draft

1st Draft

1st Draft

1st Draft

1st Draft

1st Draft

1st Draft

1st Draft

1st Draft

1st Draft

1st Draft

1st Draft

1st Draft

1st Draft

1st Draft

1st Draft

1st Draft

1st Draft

1st Draft

1ˢᵗ Draft

_____

_____

_____

_____

_____

_____

_____

_____

_____

_____

_____

_____

_____

_____

_____

_____

1st Draft

1st Draft

1st Draft

1st Draft

1st Draft

1st Draft

1st Draft

1st Draft

1st Draft

1st Draft

1st Draft

1st Draft

1st Draft

1st Draft

1st Draft

1st Draft

1st Draft

1st Draft

1st Draft

1st Draft

1st Draft

1st Draft

1st Draft

_____

_____

_____

_____

_____

_____

_____

_____

_____

_____

_____

_____

_____

_____

Section Five:
Research
and
Maps

Research

Research

Research

Research

Research

Research

Research

Research

Research

Research

Research

Research

Research

Research

Research

Research

Research

Research

Research

Research

Research

Research

Research

Research

Research

Research

Research

Research

Research

Research

Made in the USA
Las Vegas, NV
22 June 2023